The Kite Project

by Abbie Rushton

illustrated by Veronica Montoya

Saul was in his bedroom. He saw a lorry outside. Some people were unpacking boxes.

"Mum, can we meet the new family?" asked Saul.

"Yes, let's go!" said Mum.

“Welcome!” said Mum. “This is Saul.”

“It’s nice to meet you! This is Chase,” the new boy’s mum said.

“We came to look after Grandad,” said Chase’s mum. “We will stay for a while.”

“I do not need looking after!” moaned Chase’s grandad.

Saul started to giggle, but Chase didn’t.

It was time to go.

“See you, Chase,” said Saul.

Chase just gave a nod.

That weekend, Saul rode his bike to the park.

“Look!” he said. “It’s Chase and his grandad.”

Chase was playing with a kite. It swirled and whirled. He looked happy.

“Wow!” said Saul. “Your kite is cool!”

Chase grinned.

“Chase made it,” said Grandad.
“He loves kites.”

“It must be hard to make a kite,” said Saul.

“I think it’s fun,” said Chase, blushing.

Saul and his mum rode back.

"I think Chase misses his home," said Saul. "I wish I could help him feel better."

The next day, Chase was in Saul's class. Chase looked unsure about what to do.

"You can sit with me," said Saul.

At lunch, Saul found their teacher.

“I have a plan!” said Saul. “It might help Chase to settle in.”

After lunch, Mr Coe talked to the class.

"Your weekend project is to make a toy!" he said.

"We could make a kite!" said Chase. "I can teach you."

The boys spent all weekend on their kite.
Chase added streamers to the tail.

The next week, the children showed their toys.

"What a fine kite!" said Mr Coe.

Saul and Chase wanted to use their new kite. Saul's mum took them to the park. Grandad came along, too.

“I hope it will not fall,” said Saul, launching the kite.

“It will be fine,” said Chase.

The kite flew up high.

“Phew!” said Saul.

Chase beamed as the kite swooped and looped.

Make a Kite Yourself!

1. Decorate a bag.

2. Snip a hole in the end.

3. Tie string to a stick.

4. Put the stick in the bag.

5. Pull the string out of the hole.

6. Tape streamers to the bag.

Encourage students to read the instructions. If you make the kite, students will need to run so that the kite catches the wind.